HAND SHADOWS

Activity Book for Kids

This book is dedicated to the children of the world. May your hearts be full of joy.

If you enjoy the book, please consider leaving a review wherever you bought it.

Get All Our New Releases For FREE!

Sign up to our VIP Newsletter to get all of our

future releases absolutely free!

www.activitynest.org/free

CONTENTS

INTRODUCTION

LET'S GET STARTED

Are you ready to get started? The first thing you will need are your hands. Go ahead and stretch your fingers out.

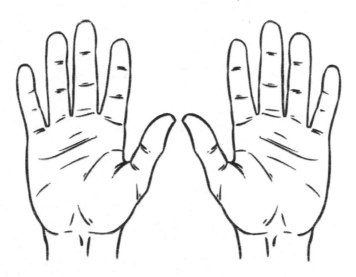

The second thing you need is a source of light. We suggest using a candle or flashlight.

BIRD

CAMEL

CAT

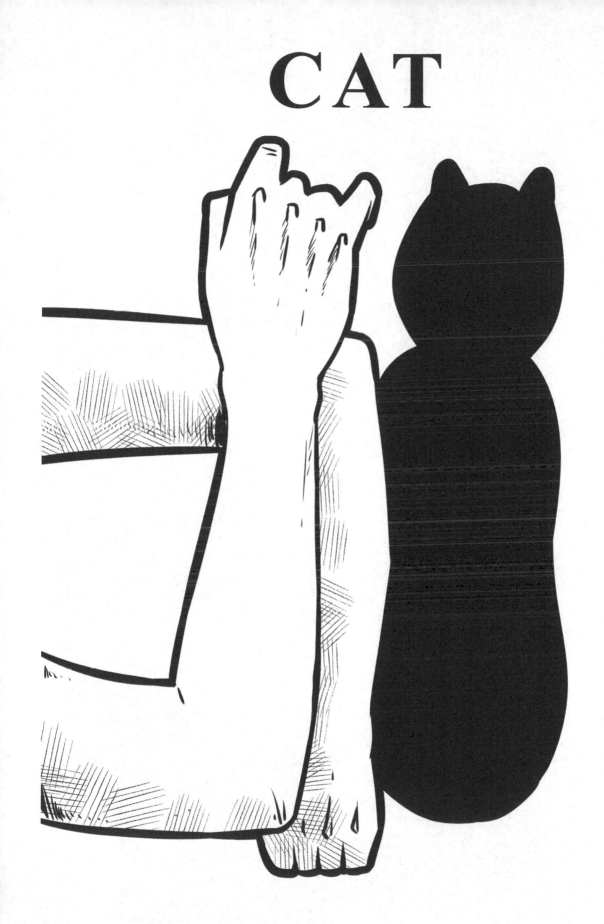

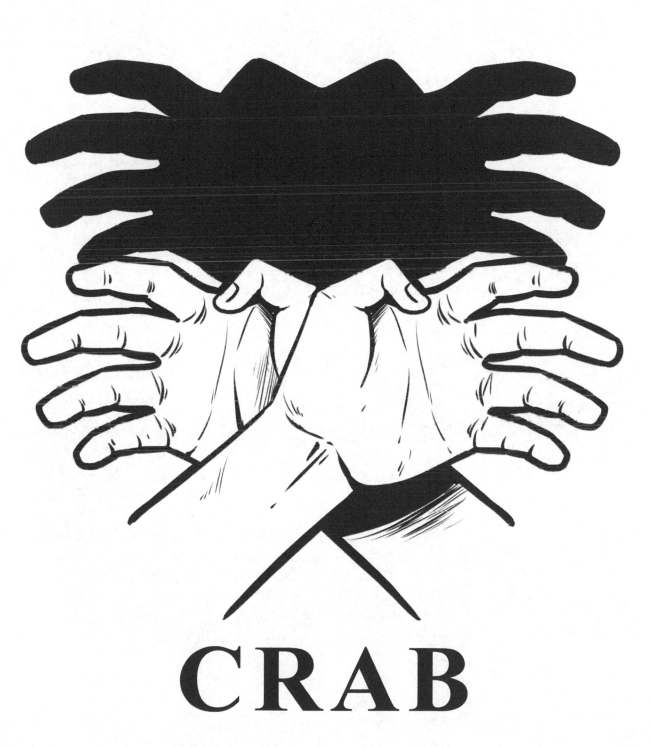

CRAB

CROCODILE

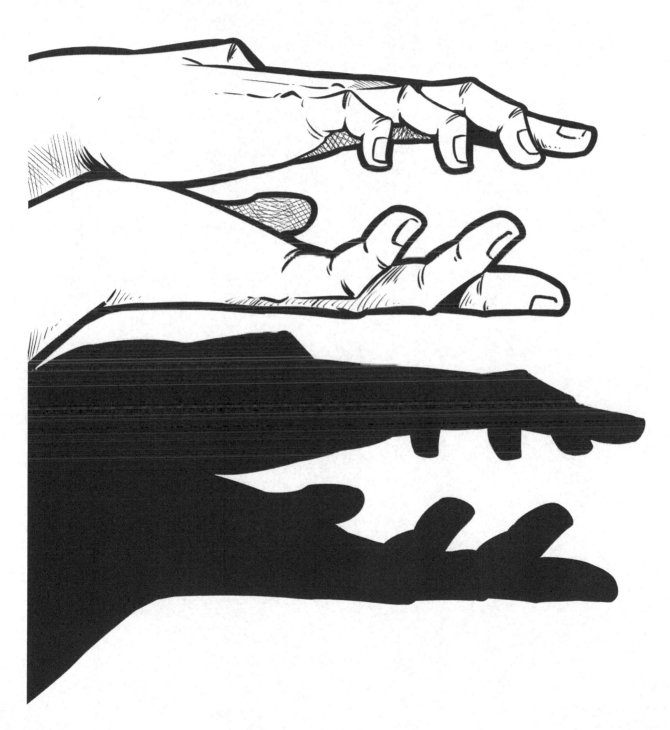

CUB

DOG

DONKEY

DUCKS

ELEPHANT

FLYING BIRD

GOAT

GOOSE

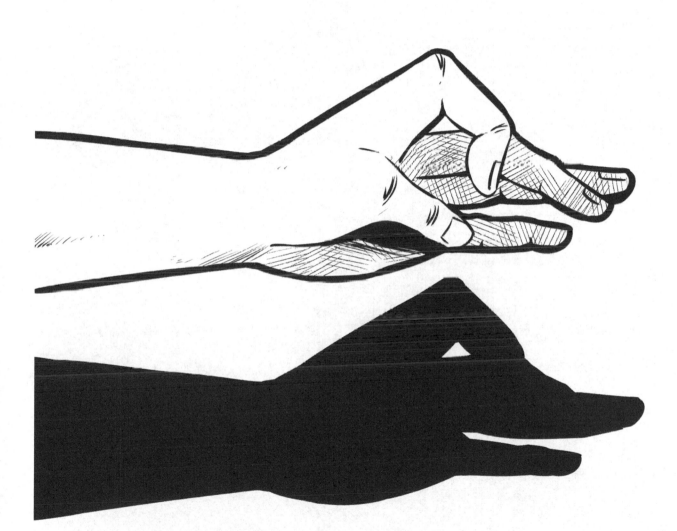

HEART

HORSE

HOUND

KANGAROO

MOOSE

OX

PANTHER

PIG

RABBIT

REINDEER

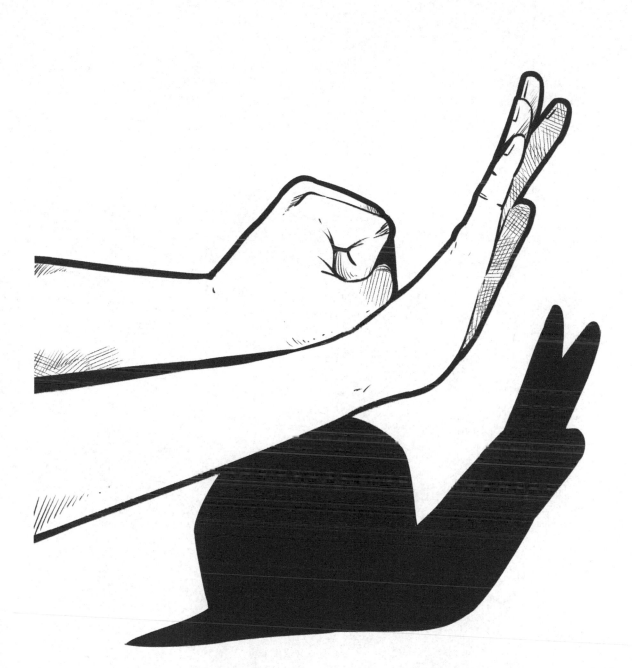

SNAIL

SPIDER

SQUIRREL

SWAN

TORTOISE

TURKEY

WOLF

THANK YOU!

Please leave us a review on Amazon.

Amazon reviews are very important to our business and help other activity lovers find our books.

Please go to this book on Amazon and let us know your honest opinion.

It would mean the world to us. Thank you!

Don't forget to sign up to our VIP Newsletter to get all of our future releases absolutely free!

www.activitynest.org/free